Enigma.

enig·ma | i-ˈnig-mə
Noun
1. something hard to understand or explain
2. a mysterious person

Trice Lashay

Copyright © 2021 Trice Foster

All rights reserved

No part of this book may be reproduced, or stored in a retrieval system, or transmitted in any form or by any means, electronic, mechanical, photocopying, recording, or otherwise, without express written permission of the publisher. For permission requests, write to the publisher, Trice Foster, via email, tricefoster@iamroyaltyet.com

Cover Design: Trice Foster

Library of Congress Control Number: 2018675309
Printed in the United States of America

This book is dedicated to...

All of the tears, all of the pain, all of the sleepless nights you will undoubtedly have to experience to become the best version of yourself. No matter what, it's worth it. It's worth it to become the person you dream of becoming.

My family and friends. Thank you for your encouragement and support. I hope having this book in your hands is tangible evidence and proof that you can do anything you set your mind to. Remove the toxicity in your life, heal your shadow self, and try. I mean really try this time. Don't give up on yourself.

My children. I can write a million books and no word in all of them could express the love I have for you. You mean everything to me. All I want is for you to believe in yourself. See yourself in the same way I see you, able, and capable of achieving whatever you set your mind to. You are beautiful souls with beautiful hearts. You are and will always be my greatest creation. Don't let this world make you forget who you are.

Sire. Thank you for helping me bring this book to life. Thank you for seeing in me what I had forgotten. Thank you for speaking life over me consistently. Thank you for being a pillar of strength in my time of weakness and vulnerability. And thank you so much for your part in my growth and healing. I'm eternally grateful.

Contents

Title Page	1
Copyright	2
Dedication	3
Preface	7
The Beginning	9
Lust	14
Toxic Patterns	29
Battle of the Mind	41
Untapped Potential	52
Growth	61
Time To Heal	71
Love	81
Spirit	94
Outspoken	103
Afterword	117
About The Author	119

Preface

Once upon a time, there was a girl who was surrounded by toxicity. She was voiceless. She didn't own who she was. And she did her best to remain unseen and out of the way. She felt like a burden and outsider, she felt alone. And even though she smiled daily. She was torn. She was a lost soul. Merely existing as a supporting role in the lives of others.

The weight of the world was too much to bear and she broke. She shattered into a thousand pieces. She inevitably died. Then...she emerged again from the broken pieces. She was a Phoenix. She shed the dust and debris of her former shell. And spread her new wings. She stood tall and a crown was bestowed upon her head. Her voice was loud and victorious.

She no longer cared to be a part of this world because she knew she was above it. She knew and owned the fact that she was different. She accepted and embraced all of herself. She blocked everything that wasn't serving her highest and truest good. She built new personal relationships with her spirit and ancestors. She listened to her inner voice.

She loved herself. Spoke affirmations over herself. She began the process of healing her shadow self. She paid attention to her heart, her body, and her spirit. And she cast out everything that didn't align with them. She lived for herself. But accepted that she was a vessel to higher consciousness for her people. She became unapologetically her. She became a free spirit. She became me.

The Beginning

"That's what people do who love you. They put their arms around you and love you when you're not so lovable." — Deb Caletti

Self Reflection

I come from a big family. Five brothers. Three sisters. Grandparents. Two moms. A dad. And then me. The middle child on my mom's side. The oldest of my dad's. Yet, I was raised as an only child. A part of everyone yet I was no one's favorite. A supporting role or extra in the lives of others. No real sense of identity or belonging.

As a child, I never had a role model. I never looked at another person in admiration, wishing I could be THAT. Come to think of it I never had someone I felt really understood me. Misunderstood my whole life, with no one to teach me how to use my voice. And so I began to write. White Sheep. Black Sheep. Outsider. Loner. Whatever you want to call me, that's who I was. And the pages of my diary became my escape.

Despite my upbringing, I always knew I was different. I always knew there was something special about me. Something divine. I will do something no one in my family has ever done. I will be great! And I will live an amazing life! I would be the one to break generational patterns and choices. I will make a way for the next generation to unlearn and relearn a new way of life! I will be the one to change the fate of our family's name! I am destined for greatness!

But I knew it would not come easy. It hasn't come easy. Failure after failure. Attempt after attempt. Choices and decisions have brought me right to this very word. This very moment. Scared out of mind. Who am I to accomplish such great feats? Who am I to do something no other person I know has done before? And can I measure up to the dreams and visions I have permanently internalized deep into the essence of who I am? Let's find out...

My Reflection

I talked to this woman who was in her late 20s. She wanted me to listen to what she had been through and had seen. The story goes she was conceived one night when her mom was drinking and her dad saw an advantage, he couldn't help but take it. My dad's a drug dealer and my mom's crack fiend. My mom treated me differently. I don't think she loves me. Connection ha! What the fuck does that mean?

My dad took care of me because my mom left me. Abandoned as a baby but my angels watched over me. She said my dad took care of me and I found a new mommy. She has been my mom since I was two. I swear she is heaven-sent. I was picked on in elementary. The kids laughed at me. Never quite fit in was even bullied.

My mom and Dad separated. There goes my family. Place to place no real sense of direction. I belong to no one, my days were so lonely. I'm thinking to myself this is such a sad story.

She said fast forward a few years later. It was me and my dad again. But it's starting to feel different. My dad is a changed man. He's hurting and he's mad. No person to call his own. The only person around is his kid and she's all grown. She'll make the perfect wife go clean up and wash my clothes. Cook for me when I get home and my food better not be cold.

You're in middle school now I bet you are messing around. Go to your room. Take off your clothes. Lay on the bed. Don't make a sound. Move your hand. Let me see. I can tell if you're messing around. Shame. Guilt. Force. Trauma. Abuse. Is her life now.

Hit! That's what you get. You should have folded my clothes. Hit! That's what you get. Blood ran from my nose. Hit! Down the steps, he knocked me down to the floor. Slap! Slap! Slap! Slap! I told you to watch the stove!

She's thinking she has to go. To heaven or somewhere close. The doors are all unlocked but there are shackles on her soul. She has no place to go. She thinks if she tells someone what happened, maybe they can save her, so she called her sister crying. Sis, I'm scared and I'm dying. I'm tired of living and tired of fighting. She left shortly after that. Never looking back.

She went to her mom's house with nothing but a sack of clothes she packed last night. Her mom said I'm sorry I know you will be alright. Someday you might forgive me. Someday you will understand. That I couldn't look you in your eyes because all I saw was your dad. But you're safe now the pain is in the past.

The next few years of her life she told me was all a blur. Drinking, smoking, doing drugs even to jail once. Amid all of the drama, she graduated high school. Then her mom snatched college from her. I'm not paying for your school. All her future dreams are gone. She was life's fool. Hope, passion, goals are all gone.

A year later she birthed a son. Her life changed from that point on. It got better with each day. She said she wasn't perfect then. And she's not perfect today. I'm listening to this woman speak with such clarity and such control. Thinking to myself how she made it only God knows.

Statistically speaking she's supposed to be dead or overdosed. She's not supposed to be telling this story or writing this poem. She's not supposed to have dreams. She's not supposed to be strong. She's not supposed to be telling me this. She's supposed to be gone. She seems so happy and vibrant. She seems so focused and clear. She seems so put together I know she handles her business.

She said I told you this story because it's not where you are from. It's about where you are going. And who you want to become. It's about loving yourself through it all. Experiences and pain. Sunshine, lighting, and rain. She said if she could do it over she'd do it over again. You see the sun blossomed me but the rain made me who I am.

She said listen don't worry about me I'm healing and moving on. And I told you this story so you can remember just how far you've come. She told me she's doing great now. Except for a few exceptions, sometimes I still talk to myself when I see my reflection.

Lust

"In my experience lust only ever leads to misery."
— Chrissie Hynde

Self Reflection

What does a young girl do when loneliness is all she has ever known? She looks for a place where she can call home. In the arms of whoever will hold her. For a moment. For an hour. Or even just for a night. What does a young woman do when every example of love and relationships, she has seen, are rooted in toxicity, dependency, drugs, violence, and infidelity? She assumes that it's normal.

Shortly after high school, with no sense of direction. I let life lead me wherever it wanted me to go. I had dreams of going to college straight from high school but that was no longer an option. So I simply wandered into scenarios, situations, and entanglements. Not knowing what I was doing. Not caring either.

I made choices. I dealt with the consequences. I accepted certain words and actions from other people that I shouldn't have. I accepted them from myself. I had no internal feelings. I was dead inside. The only love I had was for my children. Outside of them, I existed solely through physical pain and pleasure. A silent cry for help no one ever heard. No one ever knew. I learned to walk and exist in the shadows. Unheard and unnoticed. My spirit cried and screamed this isn't right! But it felt good and I enjoyed the high.

If Only You Knew

I wish you knew how important you were to me. I wish you knew I think about you almost all of my waking moments. I think about your smile. Your demeanor. How you slightly sway when you walk. I think about how soft and calm the sound of your voice is to me. Like a cool ocean breeze or the whispers of the wind.

I wonder what it is that keeps me from telling you my true emotions. What keeps me hidden behind a mask of contentment. Then again how can I ponder such a question when in my deepest of heart I know the answer. Fear. I know you don't feel as I feel so why go through the agonizing pain of rejection. Why kill myself inside?

I can't tell you how it came to this why or when. All I know is what is. And the truth is I am in love with you. I wish I could tell you that. I wish I could tell you, you make my heart smile. I wish I could tell you that I don't want to be with anybody else except you. I wish I wasn't alone in my thoughts.

I wish this wasn't so…how could I be in love with you. It's not the right time. You're not the right person. I asked my spirit guides and guardian angels to assist me on this journey of love and lead my heart in such a way that the next person I fall in love with will be my soulmate. I don't know, maybe we were close in a past life.

I don't know what to think about you. I don't know what to feel. I don't even know if I want to call this love. Maybe it's the connection we have shared on several occasions that have bound our souls together.

Maybe it's infatuation. Lust. Maybe it's the fact that I've gotten used to you being around. You're a consistent part of my life. I had been searching for consistency in someone. Anyone. And you were the first to give it to me. So what is this feeling? Is it worth telling you? Is it worth the risk? I wish I knew and if I did I would tell you. So many what-ifs come to mind. It's hard to get them all out at once.

What if you don't feel the same way? What if you do? Then what. Where would we go from there? What if it doesn't last? What if we don't work? How far could we go? How deep could we get? What would be the effects on the world if we were together? What would we create? Peace or chaos? Would I come out a better woman? Will my children be positively or negatively affected by our choice? Family? Friends? Can I love you? Will you let me? Or will you shut me out? Can you love me? Do you even know how to love?

Maybe I could teach you how to love me. Maybe you can do the same for me. We could be in this together. Against all odds. It would be a story to tell. But…you'll never know. And I will never find out the answer to any of these questions. For now, they are thoughts in my head. Visions in my mind's eye. Simply words on a blank page…

My Addiction

Damn baby, what am I to do with you? I mean what can I do with myself? I'm a mess. I'm strung out on you and you love it. I hate that I need you. Loathe that I want you. I despise the fact that I'm hooked on your sex. Logic leaves me. I breathe you. I inhale you. Exhale you. I breathe deep.

I love it when your skin touches mine. I love to feel your legs against my thighs. You open me as I invite you in. Your lips against my neck. Your hands search my body. With each touch, I lose control. I'm a mess. I can't help myself. My mind is no longer with me. I act on pure lust and passion. Raw emotions take over.

Your energy is so high. You're mine. Cloud nine. Cloud ten. Again. And again. And again. To think about it is to feel you. Forever etched in my memory. Your scent is a part of my sheets. I remember you going deep. My knees go weak. I can't speak. Just breathe. As flashbacks make my body weak.

Damn it, I'm a mess. But I need it and I want it. And I want you to want me. So I breathe deep. You take me there. Every time. I want you to feel me. I want you to hear me. Every breath. Every scream. Every whimper. Every cry. It's been a long time. Forever and a day. Don't make me wait. Don't make me beg. Baby please, whatever you say. Just give me more of you.

All that is me is yours. Every pore opens up to allow you to come close. I'm so close. Don't stop. Just keep going. Overdose. I've lost control. And you know it. You love it. I need you please don't go. Be with me.

I've heard stories of sins feeling so good they have to be right. But you take the cake and you bite. And lick and you slurp and you eat and swallow all that is me. Disbelief. You devour the whole piece.

Still, there is hunger in your eyes. And the only thing that can satisfy your needs is me. And the only thing that can get me high is you. So we entwine. And our souls connect through our eyes. Bodies connect through the passage between my thighs. Yes, I am yours and you are mine. Damn, I'm so high. But still though just one more time...

Forbidden Desire

Desire. Sweet, hot soul burning desire. You're poison, you know that? A sin in your being. And you don't even know it. Maybe you do. You're my luscious forbidden fruit. I yearn for you. I want to feel your mocha skin entwined in mine. I lick my lips and I think about what you taste like.

I want to kiss you and feel the depths of your soul on the tip of my tongue. I want to feel my senses heighten as electricity pulsate through me. Only you could do it. I've always longed for you. Wishin for one night, I could play on your senses, tease you, taunt you, and tantalize you until you become weak with as much lust as you've given me.

I wonder if you have noticed me. Have you felt me undressing you piece by piece, slow and steady with my eyes? Pleasing you in the only way I can...in my mind? I'm in love with your body. The way you walk, powerful yet controlled. The way you speak with such engaging intellect.

To see you smile is to feel myself become aroused. To feel you close to me is to wish you were closer. And to watch you leave or say goodbye is to take a piece of me with you. I regret feeling like this. You're so off-limits. But I regret that in that instant I didn't tell you what I wanted you to hear. I didn't show you what I wanted you to see. No words amongst us could express how much I want to confess my lust for you.

How would you take it? Would you comply with my wishes and release all inhibitions? Would you live in the moment as I wish to do? Would you keep it a secret or confess it to the world? Would you turn your back on me, leaving me with a shattered pride?

I can only imagine. For now, I'll leave my fantasies at rest, locked in the deepest crevices of my mind. And I'll pretend, that is until you give me a sign. And I'll wear this mask of conformity you've grown so accustomed. Maybe someday I will swallow my pride. Tell you how I feel. Tell you what I think. I'll conjure up the courage to tell you my one true fantasy. The fantasy that for the life of me I can't seem to shake. No matter how many times I remind myself of just how wrong it is.

I know if given the opportunity I would readily jump on it, pun intended. But for now, I will play along, seeping in the thoughts of you. Wishing, yearning, and hoping for just one chance. Why just one chance? Because, my little secret, I know that is all it would take.

Drugs and Poison

Cyanide kiss. Baby, you're deadly. You are toxic and you know it. But I will allow you to kill me softly and slowly and gently because it feels so good. I don't know what it is about you. Could it be your tantalizing eyes or your infamous vibe? Whatever it is, I'm trying to catch your wave and ride that ride. I'm hooked. Addiction taking over every realm of my being.

I need it. I need you. Like the first dose of heroin through a virgin's arm. You are my fix. And I want your life and existence to flow through my veins. You're like cold fire. You keep my insides aflame while the skin of my flesh remains chilled.

Cold sweat. You see baby I'm raining wet, no I'm drenched and soaked and it's all your fault. How you rock this boat. Damn that stroke. How you stay afloat because anyone else would drown in this ocean. You cause me to scream and my sounds evaporate on your tongue.

I can feel myself letting go, I can feel myself losing control. I can feel myself grabbing hold...to any strand of sanity I have left. To no avail. I fail. And just like that, it's gone. And so are my inhibitions. So are all my thoughts and all of my feelings. I have nothing left inside. The past is gone. There is no future. And I am only here presently yours.

The serpent's tongue tastes this apple. Your venom spreads through me like a wildfire. The touch of my skin connecting and entangling in yours is enough to send me over the edge. Baby, you're cyanide. If pleasure is truly pain then I have died a thousand times.

I scream. I moan. I whine. I cry. What have I done to deserve this agonizing pleasure? I'll do it again. And again. Pleasure this good has to be a sin. But this feeling I'm feeling and I'm feeling it deep. And I'm feeling it grow is only pleasing me. So don't stop. Just go. Harder and deeper.

You've ignited the fire. You're hot, I'm sweating. Burning in this fire. I won't turn back. My flesh is smoking. And your eyes. So menacing. So deep. So intense. Let me know you're not to be fucked with. I know this was your plan all along. I know you wanted this moment. You're so toxic. You knew just one dose of your poison. Your venom. Your drug. And I would be hooked. I would no longer be myself. And now I am lost in your daze. Your hypnotic ways connect with these aquatic waves.

This is not me. I'm not here. I'm with you. I belong to you. I am your slave. Your mistress, your addict. And for that moment you are my master and my addiction. And I crave more. I'm ravenous and insatiable. So give it to me now. Give me more. I don't care if it's wrong I need to feel the effects of your sex again. I need to go for that ride. I need that high. Cyanide baby, you're cyanide.

Written Seduction

Ok see this part right here is really 'bout to be the move. And I'm about to see how many words I can use to get you in the mood. And you're seeing how I can flow you oughta watch how I can groove. See by the end of this poem you'll be begging for round two.

Now we gone take this tempo up a few notches. This ain't a peep show but I don't care who's watching. And don't try to tell me no now cuz it ain't no stopping. And nah I ain't Chris but watch how I can get it poppin'. And you say you can pick it up but first watch how I drop it.

Now let me open up wide and put my lips around it. Make your dick touch my throat go in and out and pound it. Nah I still ain't finished yet but I like how this is sounding. And you'll be still feeling the effects of this poem in the morning. Now I'm warning you baby you best take caution cuz I will have you dizzy light-headed moaning and groaning. Don't back down when Pandora's box is finally open.

And when you're ready for me I'll be more than just focused. Honey, I'm hardly joking. Call it Facebook fucking we gone do some serious poking. And I'ma pacify you baby yea some serious sucking. Catching squirrel orgasms yes some serious nuttin. Nah I still ain't finished yet and already you lusting. But until we meet again this is just my written seduction.

Now you're excited you know what I want you to do for me now. Relax your mind, close your eyes. Play like you going down south. Spread your fingers open it wide now stick your tongue out. Make your lips touch my lips now that's mouth to mouth. Rainforest pussy baby no such thing as a drought. And we'll see who's the real fighter when I give you this total knockout.

I know what you're thinking, did she say what I think she said. I must be trippin cuz she couldn't have wrote what I think I read. Food for thought so consider your fantasy finally fed. And it ain't over I ain't done this just the tip of the head. How 'bout I take you to my room, show what you're missing instead. Baby, it's yours like a late-night special that's red.

Hold up ain't it crazy how I'm using the words that I'm using. Doing so much seducing your belt buckle is loosening. And I will put your ass to sleep with all the moves I am doing. And you can tell me you don't feel it but come on who are you fooling? Okay, I'm almost done by now you should be feenin. By now you should be thinking of ways to make this pussy cream. And I know I've given you something you're not used to. Now follow me to my bedroom this is to be continued...

Torn Asunder

Day falls and the night rises
The sun is down but the moon is shining
It's cold outside but temperatures keep rising
As I find myself fantasizing about you
And yes it may be true
That the man that I'm with is no longer you
I can't help but think about what I once knew
Can't help but to feel what I felt was real
You see this man, his power, his strength, his name
May have my body but what you have he could never obtain
He has my legs my thighs my innermost parts
But what you have is my heart
And all that is mine
From the secrets of my soul to the memories of my mind
My experiences my past my love my pain
As he thrusts inside of me again and again
The I love you's and I miss you's
Turn into I want to just do you no better yet just fuck you
And my body's lost in ecstasy but I just want you next to me
My body sinning uncontrollably but my heart cries faithfully
And patiently awaiting the
Day in which you come back and tell me I can have that
I mean I can have this, this is that sweet kiss
That *if I had one wish* kiss
The day in which you come back and tell me you're still mine
But I guess I'll have to wait endlessly until next time

An Ode to My Forbidden Love

I never thought I would be writing this. I never thought I'd be writing it to you. Then again since when was the mind capable of foreseeing the future. You know I think about you from time to time. Reminiscing on the way things were. Wondering what could have been. Trying to figure out just why it didn't.

What happened that altered the outcome of our future? It's funny how time changes all....even funnier how we never seem to notice to what extent those changes occur. That is until it's too late. And we are left there confused and bewildered, forced in our will and fate to accept reality. A reality we never saw coming.

While I can only accept these changes...I wonder if you think of me? Do you reminisce on what was? Do you miss the laughter we shared? Do you miss being able to talk and lend an open ear? Do you miss the moments? Does this ode make you miss me even a little? Do you yearn for just one more moment in which everything you could have said...everything you could have done...there was a chance to? Does it pain you knowing that chance will never come? Can you live with it...

It's unbearable, isn't it? Wishing you could have done more and said more. Maybe just maybe things would be different...and now look at our present. Gone. Everything is gone. Gone is the laughter we once shared. Gone are the moments we spent together. Closeness is gone. Friendship is gone. Time is gone. And we have gone our separate ways. We were Romeo and Juliet. You were my forbidden love. Sinful fruit. With each kiss, I fell deeper. With each touch, a part of me was given to you. And each time our bodies connected my sanity was altered. I permitted you to lead me into the abyss.

And what's left? Memories, bittersweet distant memories. Memories that seem to fade with each passing day. Until a moment, a smell, a sound, a touch, a word takes me back down memory lane. And then I smile. Forgive me for this is the only way I can speak clearly to you. My thoughts on paper. My emotions bleed through my pen, with each stroke I continue to reminisce. Once upon a time, you told me you loved me. I wonder was it true? Is it still true today? We will never know. But sometimes I can be caught remembering, reminiscing on what was, yet grateful for what will never be. I'm happy to have you as simply a distant memory.

Toxic Patterns

" There's the idea that love is supposed to hurt, but it really shouldn't hurt." — Elizabeth Lail

Self Reflection

What is it? What keeps me going back? Peace and healing are waiting for me in the comfort of my home. And still, I choose pain? I choose confusion, doubt...passion. It feels good. But it hurts. I'm so stupid. Here I go giving myself to pain again.

You would think I would have learned my lesson by now. You would think on the outside looking in that maybe I could grasp the concept of picking the right men to fall in love with. Several areas of life and this by far has been the most unsuccessful. I don't know why I always fall in love with the wrong ones.

But again it feels good. Like a drug. I'm high on his supply. I need it. I crave it. My judgment is clouded. It'll work this time. I know it will. I have a feeling. He'll change this time. He never changes...

But the memories, I could have sworn, they were all good. And the bad times, they weren't so bad. Of course, they were bad. They were the worst. I cried the majority of the time. Wondering why he couldn't see how much pain he caused me...but I could have sworn...

Eventually, the story will end the same. I keep thinking it's something wrong with me. I mean it has to be me right? Something about me attracts the broken and unhealed. Maybe I am broken and unhealed.

I dont know. I'm confused. Disgruntled. I know what I should do... stay single. FOREVER! Who has time to wonder if the person you're in love with is really in love with you. I mean how could you go forward with your day carrying baggage that clouds your thoughts and emotions all day? It's absurd really.

But I don't. I take the chance. I turn the flicker into a raging fire. I'm in hell right now. But it feels good. Passion. Fire. Lust. Love. Confusion. Thirst. Hunger. Pain. Lies. I'm in love with it all. Go ahead, tell me more lies. Make me feel less than I am. Fill me with your demons. I can take the pain.

What did I just do? Why didn't I stop? Why did I go? Why didn't I leave? What happens next? What do I do now? Enjoy the flames...I'll deal with the scars in the morning.

Feelings. Emotions. Guilt. Vulnerability. You know the crazy thing is I don't have a problem with being vulnerable. I don't have a problem with sharing to the world the emotions I go through daily. Writing has always been an outlet to me so I write about it. One day though, all of this is going to be worth it. One day I'll write my own happily ever after. I'll make all the pain worth it. So I continued to write.

Love's Sin

What does it mean to be in love? Does anyone know? Can you tell me? If not, then can I ask what is love exactly? I mean the meaning of love itself. Many years ago, I assumed love was but an illusion. A figment of one's imagination. Smoke light and mirrors. A chemical imbalance if you will. At last, I have, through my many years of experience, found it to be much more than it seems.

This is love's hidden agenda. This is love's sin. Love is an addiction. It is known to be the light in our darkness but the unspoken truth is it can also be the darkness that kills the light within us. Those who have seen this darkness will understand.

The thing about love is...it is blinding. Neurologically speaking it is a real addiction. Therefore those that are in the cusps of its magnitude and are in detrimental relationships do not see the misery they are keeping because they are too busy looking and searching for the high of the new love they experienced earlier in the relationship.

Only the strong-minded and self-aware can see what's wrong and make a conscious decision to break the addiction. The weak are those who choose to stay despite all of the pain, detriment, and hindrance it causes them. Confusing loyalty with ignorance and love with emotional, physical, and psychological dependency.

If it's lost you abandon all inhibitions and go after it. Day after day, night after lonely, desperate night. Seeking, yearning, craving that first high only to be disappointed. This is nothing like before. What happened to the first high of new love? What was once love in your heart is replaced by lust in the flesh. And it is unfulfilling, degrading, and shameful. But you say you've found love, you even make yourself believe you've found it.

You know something is missing. Something is not right. You begin to question yourself. You question your sanity. Could you ever feel again? Could you ever experience true love? You become a victim of love using its name in vain. Cursing, blaming, resenting, despising the whole nature and actions behind the word. You hate it. Look at what love did to you! Look what it made you do! Love provided a home for the demons you now have inside of you. You loathe the person that did this to you. You hate their love. And you hate yourself for loving them.

How could you have been so stupid? How could you have been so dumb? How could you have been so weak? So vulnerable? What kind of sick person would do this to themselves? Love has ruined you with its drug. But you go back to your supplier. Over and over again. Their love is so addicting. To be away, to even try to be strong you risk withdrawals…it hurts too much to leave. Hurts too much to stay. So you hold on to it for dear life.

You don't want to forget. You don't want to move on. But you must. Too many memories. You miss the times, you miss the laughter, you miss the hurt, you miss the pain. You miss the tears. You miss the flutter in your heart every time they were near. It kills you slowly from the inside out. Disintegrating your heart. Shattering your spirit. Until you become a shell. A shell of your former being. So you can't go back, you can't relapse. It's too dangerous. So you push it. You push it deep down in the crevices of your soul. Hoping it is not revealed. Hoping people don't see the scars from love's addiction.

Repeated Patterns

I can't breathe. You suffocate me. I'm weak. Deep down I know we can never be. I try. Because I've been alone for so long. By my lonesome. I'm lonely. It's corny, I know. But it is what it is. I'm tired of lying to myself. I don't want to lie to myself anymore. My head hurts and my heart's sore. And it's all because I put my trust in you. I put my love in you. I put my time in you. And when you don't come through. I'm lost. In my head, I keep thinking again and again. Why do I keep coming back to peace interrupted? You're so emotionally destructive. But I drown in your seduction. This has to be just lust. Because I can't imagine that this is enough. That this is all there is to love.

But I'm weak. You say stay. I don't leave. I shout. You laugh. My pain, your laughter. You keep living while I die a little inside. And I believe my own lies. Silent cries. Tears you will never see. I wept on my pillow before I went to sleep. And I pray. I pray I learn the lesson. I gain strength. I gain the clarity to know when enough is enough. I wake up. I act dumb. And I swallow my pride and swallow the lies you tell me and yourself because I see the potential in us. I'm blinded. Smoke and mirrors. It's all fake, this is not the life I imagined. I'm insane. But you made me his way. And you know it's true. And the sad truth is you don't even really want to be with me, you just don't want me to be with anyone but you.

Don't Lie To Me

Last night you told me you love me. But you knew I was upset. You knew it was a possibility that I wouldn't want to be with you. You were afraid that I may leave. So I asked you much later did you mean it. "I wouldn't have said it if I didn't mean it. I never intended for you to be mad. I just wanted to be honest." I know. I believe you.

As many times as I want to walk away. As many times as I doubt this will even last. Something keeps me here. Some part of me wants to keep fighting. And see what's on the other side. What's in our future. Something deep inside me wants to help you be more than you are. I see the potential in you. I know you want to be better. Then again I may be losing it. But isn't that what love is. Insanity. Actions without reason. Feelings without logic.

But I'm sorry I can't say it. Not right now. Not like this. I'm afraid. Saying it makes it real. Saying it gives you control. Saying it makes me vulnerable. I'm so afraid that you'll hurt me. I'm afraid you'll make me cry. I'm afraid you won't love me as much as I do you. You won't care for me as I do you. I'm afraid you won't give me what I need from you. Constant reassurance. Maybe you will lie. Maybe you will cheat. Maybe you'll become disrespectful and deceitful. Maybe this is all a game to you, maybe you don't take me seriously. Maybe you just said it to secure your position.

I tend to overthink. What if you leave me? Then again is love not taking chances. Is love not the biggest risk of them all. I won't say it though... not yet. God knows I can't take more heartache. I can't take more let down. So please catch me now before I fall in love with you and say it too.

Silent Wishes

I wish I didn't feel the way I feel about you
Wish that I knew what to do
Wish I wasn't so confused

I wish I can get you out of my head
Wish some word were never said
Wish I could make you understand

I wish you didn't mean this much to me
Wish you weren't all I need
Wish I could make you see

I wish I didn't feel this way
Wish you would go away
Wish you would stay

I wish I didn't want you to hold me tight
Wish you didn't make me cry
Wish I could say goodbye

I wish I could say no to you
I wish I could say I'm through
Wish I never met you

I wish I didn't feel this hurt
Wish I didn't give a fuck
Wish I didn't love you so much…but I do

Tired

I'm tired of loving unconditionally
Just so he can lash out uncontrollably
And tell me he loves me as well
That is until good times fail
Then he's off, no trail
Leaving behind just my broken heart
Shattered dignity pail of tears
I'm tired of giving my all
Staying loyal when he falls
Toxic love withdrawals
I'm tired of tired excuses
And me playing dumb
I'm tired of being lonely in my own home
Tired of feeling alone
I'm tired of calling when you're gone
You don't pick up the phone
I'm tired of all the lies
I'm tired of all the crying
I'm tired of fake goodbyes
I'm tired of forgiving you once again
I'm tired of maybe we should just be friends
Somebody, please save me I'm tired of being the savior
I'm tired of this cape where is superman when you need him
I'm done trying, fighting, and crying
And we all know what happens to a woman
When she is finally tired.

Love's Lessons

It wasn't meant for me to fall in love with the wrong one...yet again.
You see for years I've been blinded and misguided, hypnotized by love's lies.
I could never see the lesson behind it.
But now I see that's what's meant to be will be in the end.
And there are never really endings, just new beginnings.
New chapters in our lives.
But to understand the book you have to read the same page a couple of times.
I guess that's life.
And now I can't tell if I'm in the same book, a different chapter, or a new book with a happily ever after.
But I do know that after this last one, I promise I'll be more careful.
I promise not to be my own antagonist.
It's 2:30 in the morning and I'm probably babbling.
But I know I'm changing and evolving, my old perspectives have dissolved.
I'm no longer longing for a calling or message in a bottle.
I'm just here to live my life. I pray to God I get it right.
Story of my life in this book I write.
But y'all don't hear me I mean y'all not listening.
Nah, y'all ain't reading.
Y'all don't feel me. One thing for sure I truly believe it.
The Goddess is at rest but she is still in me.

No Longer Blind

They say it is better to have loved and lost than to have never loved at all. But the loves of my past I believe were my downfall. My Grandma always said Dede, don't give a man your all. So in the public eye, I refused to cry. I stood tall. Don't get me wrong for accepting the pain and ignoring the red flags, this is my fault. I know I am not weak but sometimes I feel small.

You see I gave them life and they took mine from me. Tried my hardest to be a future wife without a ring silly me. Would they ever do the same for me? Probably not. I was blinded. Call it soul ties. I was bonded. While trying to save them. I lost myself.

I was so focused on what I wanted. The perfect couple for just a moment. That I was distracted from the essentials I desperately needed. And slowly but surely I became weak. The woman in the mirror is no longer me. Deep inside I am better than what is seen.

They say love makes you stupid. Love makes you blind. But the ignorance really lies in the lines of repetitive lies. So wrapped up in the image of the mind. Never realizing what illusions our heart plays on our eyes. I was hypnotized and mesmerized by toxic love's lies.

I always see potential. A small blessing in a deeply rooted curse. I kept trying to find the good. They kept showing me their worst. Actions speak louder than words. I should have listened to me first.

But you see the power of love is stronger than the purest drug. Inside I knew I should leave but I'd rather self-destruct. So I hid the pain. Covered the shame. Swallowed my pride. Play the game. I closed my eyes. I rolled the dice. Prayed multiple times. Damn... snake eyes. It saddens me. That I only wanted to help. I wanted to be there. But in the midst of trying to save them...I forgot to save myself.

Battle of the Mind

"My demons, inner strengths, and physical battles have guided me through life." — GG Allin

Self Reflection

Damn it! I wish I wasn't afraid of my own strength. I wish I wasn't afraid to leap. I wish I could do what I know I need to do. I don't know what's wrong with me. Why can't I be the woman I know I am meant to be?

What's it going to take for me to get it? What's it going to take for me to move? What's it going to take for me to take action! How can someone who quite literally possesses the blueprint to their success not see to it that it is manifested?

It's not like I think I can't do it. Is it laziness? Is it a lack of willpower? Lack of confidence? Lack of motivation? It can't be, because I don't just want it! I crave it! I yearn for it! I dream about it! I talk about it! I think about it! I've planned for it! I pray for it! Speak affirmations over it!

I do everything except take the action steps… I guess it's better to live in my head than in real-life. I wish I could wake up tomorrow and be the woman who goes after what she wants and doesn't stop until it's hers! I'm so torn between the person I have always been and the woman I know I was meant to be. Battle of the mind I suppose…or maybe I'm depressed. Maybe I'm crying for help.

Babblin

I have to get this out in the open.
I can't hold it.
Sometimes I feel like smoking.
Pulling the trigger till there's nothing but smoke.
Sometimes I feel like drinking or drowning,
Or emptying a bottle of pills till I'm drowsy.
I know what you're thinking but you're doing so good.
No, I'm not, I can't stop the voices!
If I could I'd do it.
It's like a million and one thoughts daily with no action.
I should have been a writer no I should have been famous.
All of these words whispering and mumbling.
I can't hear myself think, my thoughts are all jumbled.
And I don't know how much more control I am under.
I don't know whether I'm lonely or want to be alone.
You don't know what I've done.
I'm here but my mind is long gone.
I can hear the skeletons still trapped in my closet.
Pandora's box has yet to be opened.
You'd leave me if you found out all the wrong I've done.
But I'm not a bad person.
Just the cards I was drawn.
The decisions I've made.
The lessons I've learned.
I'm in a constant battle with who I was who I am
And who I'm trying to become.
And all of them have voices.
All of them have words.
All of them have memories and scars that still hurt.
One is wishing I'd speak up.
One is wishing I'd fight.

One has secrets and shadows she's always trying to hide.
All I want is a chance to be free.
But how do I free my higher self when my subconscious has the key.
I know I'm destined for greatness.
It's all about the collective.
The story of an old soul.
The journey of an earth angel.
The world's pain on my shoulders.
Their well being at heart.
Want to reach my destiny I don't know where to start
Or what to do I'm so confused.
I don't want to lose.
I'm stuck in the same book, just different chapters.
I'm slowly giving up on my happily ever after.
Don't mind me though I'm probably just babblin…

Troubled Soul

What do you do when you want to cry but your pride won't let you? There are no more tears left. What do you do when everything seems to be crushing you. You're tired of being strong. You're fighting a losing battle. No more fight left in you. No more strength to keep yourself together.

The mask starts to fall off and you can no longer hide behind happiness that doesn't exist. Whatever this is I feel it. I don't want to feel anymore. I don't know what to do or what to say. I feel so far from myself. I wonder how did I allow this to happen to me?

I don't want to cry anymore. I don't want to be sad anymore. I don't want to think myself into sleepless nights. Wondering what I should say. A million words I never said eat away at my consciousness. But how do I express myself? A million things to say but I haven't found my voice. A million steps to take but am I strong enough to take the first one?

How do I express how hurt I am? How tired I am. Confused. Troubled. Depressed. Who can I call who can I run to? Who will console me? Who will be there for me? I need a shoulder. A lap. A warm chest. An ear. I need someone to care...

You're Not Alone

A lot of people don't understand it. It's hard to explain.
As much love as you give you still feel the pain.
As much light as you spread you still feel the rain.
Feels like a thousand pounds on you. You feel empty inside.
But you can't let them see you down because of your pride.
If I told you I was good and everything is okay, man I lied.
Deep inside I feel broken and I'm just tired of hiding.
To be honest I'm struggling too. Struggling with bills and the rent.
Struggling with having enough energy to be a mom at her best.
Struggling with finding peace and joy even though I'm in debt.
I'm struggling with feeling alone. Struggling to make a home.
Struggling to find a way to raise two kids on my own.
Struggling to work this nine to five and I'm blessed that I have it,
While it's people scamming and fucking their way to a sack.
Mentally and emotionally I feel drained like I'm drowning.
I can't eat, I can't sleep, I'm losing the ability to function.
I feel weak.
The longer the nights grow the more my days turn bleak.
And it's cold in my heart. Dark thoughts in my head.
Would my children be better off if I was in jail or dead?
Maybe my kids will do better with another person instead.
Maybe I'm not fit. Maybe it's too much.
Maybe I'm fooling myself with fake blessings and luck.
Swear to God most times I feel like just not giving a fuck!
But then I get on my knees God I'm here help me, please.
Let the tears fall while I cry, my heart bleeds.
Do angels answer prayers if so I'm down here pleading!
What have I done that's so wrong why is this happening to me?
What did I do wrong? Why am I being punished like this?
Look at the sky then at my wrist. At the knife and then I twitch.
It could all be so simple I can take the pain away...

God these thoughts in my head please take them all away.
I don't want to die inside. I truly want to stay.
I want to be a good mom. I want to remain strong.
But it's only so much I can take. Just hold me close in your arms.
On behalf of those who are hurting.
God please don't let us down. Don't let us lose sight of our dreams.
Don't let our demons win. I still have faith in the end.
Don't let our life be in vain.
Don't let the light within us be cast out by darkness and pain.
Help us endure all the tests that we have been given.
God, please help us remember that all our lives are worth living.

Alter Ego

I am broken...
How can I truly be loved?
If I don't know how to love in return.
I am a wilted rose in an engulfing flame
Beautiful, dark, mesmerizing, and hypnotic
I am said to be light in the abyss of darkness
But I am also a depleting reservoir
The energy I have taken
Pain disappointment confusion despair
It's too much to bear.
Yet I wear it comfortably
How could you dare to fall for this unwarranted connection?
You were warned and yet you chose to satisfy your curious nature.
Be careful.
She is a black widow.
Hidden, menacing, enticing, and waiting.
Walk away before you are webbed in her emotional lies and false sense of connection.
You'll look into her eyes and see the reflection of everything you ever wanted.
I will if you let me. And she will take over.
And it will feel so good. So deep. So passionate.
You will be ignited. Intoxicated. Drugged in my love and you will be mine.
I didn't choose this.
Out of the darkest crevices of my past
She was born. This is who I have become.
I nurse her. Carry her. Let her consume me.
I am ravenous and insatiable.
She loves it. I cry.

She thrives. I die.
Each time it is done.
We are one.
I am.
Sasha.

Shadow Work

Who am I?
I am everything you want to hide.
And nothing you want to keep.
I thrive in the pits of hell from which I was created.
I'm the blood you've tasted.
And everything you loathe and hate.
You can say all my motives are premeditated.
I'm in every reflection you don't want to see.
I'm in your shadow lurking
And in your mind's eye smirking.
I know what you did last night.
I am brimstone and fire.
Lust and desire.
The illusions in your mirror
Where there's rage there I am.
Deny me if you want, that's how my fire is fed.
But you can't ignore all the whispers I've said
I am every skeleton in your closet.
Every secret you've ever kept.
I'm the voices in your head.
The fear that makes you sweat,
And makes your heart race,
And makes your soul shake.
I'm every crime you've ever committed.
Drugs and money, sex and poison
I am the vibrations, changes, and energy exchanges of every demon you've allowed to live here.
Don't worry I'm hidden waiting patiently,
Behind closed doors.
But I'll be there when the mask falls off.
You can't run from me. You can't hide.

All you can do is keep ME hidden.
But for how long?
They call me evil.
But it's two sides to every story.
I am merely the consequence of every betrayal,
Every heartache. Every injustice. Every failure.
Who am I?
Every dark side to your fantasies and fables.
I am you…but,
They call me the Devil.

Untapped Potential

"…because once you discover yourself and accept what you are, then you can fulfill your true potential and be happy." — Marco Pierre White

Self Reflection

There have been plenty of times when I've held myself back from great opportunities and advancements. I've lost possible friendships, relationships, partnerships, and connections not putting my whole self out there.

There have been times when I should have spoken up. I should have done more. There were times when I should have followed my intuition and took action right then and there.

But I didn't. I don't know why. I truly believe I am destined for greatness. I truly believe I was put here as a servant to others. I am meant to achieve great things and I am meant to help as many as I can along this journey. And somehow make life a little better than before I came into it. I KNOW THIS.

But deep down, like a whisper in the distance. Very faintly, there is some doubt. I can hear a very small part of me...maybe my inner child... asking...can I be all that is expected of me? Am I really capable? Do I have what it takes to become the woman I've dreamt of being?

Surely it wouldn't be in my spirit to be if I wasn't worthy right? I know I can't keep living like this and I KNOW at some point SOMETHING WILL change inside of me. And I know one day I will FINALLY be in alignment with who I am inherently supposed to be. I KNOW I will. Just like I know I can't continue missing out on life by being my own worst hindrance. And like I KNOW I can't die with all of who I am still invisible to the world.

I guess the question is how can I silence that little voice? Not just silence but remove completely?? And why is it so hard for me to just BE instead of wishing, hoping, praying, and waiting to become?

I have to remember that I am enough. I have enough. I know enough to start. That's all I have to do. Start. One step in front of the other. One word after the next. And just like that, I have accomplished myself as a published writer! It could have all been so simple.

But my mind plays its little tricks. The little voice inside my head. "You're not ready. You're not good enough. The timing is off." NOT THIS TIME MIND! Not this time FEAR. Not this time DOUBT. I AM READY. I AM GOOD ENOUGH. I AM NOT AFRAID. AND THE TIME IS RIGHT NOW!

I had to. I needed to. I couldn't have lived with myself if I didn't. So often we are caught in preparation mode. I should tweak this. I should try that. I should learn more. Go to school. Go to training. Become certified. We get stuck in the double dutch mode of life. About to jump but never leaping.

I was tired of telling people what I was about to do. I was tired of people getting excited for me only to fall short of my promises. Most of all, I was tired of looking in the mirror knowing I can be, do, have, and say so much more. I was tired of letting myself down.

I am tired. I'm tired of being this watered-down version of who I am inside! The only thing separating me from who I am and who I want to become is the actions I take from this moment on. I can not...I refuse to let this momentum diminish. This time I'm going after everything I want!

Who Am I?

I'm too conscious for the ones who'd rather sleep,
Yet I don't know enough for the woke ones.
I'm too spiritual for Christians,
Yet I don't meditate enough to be spiritually awakened.
I'm too quiet to be labeled cool,
Yet even the misfits have a crowd.
I care enough about the world,
Yet I'm just not into politics.
I don't have enough money to walk with the elite,
Yet, I dare not claim to struggle in poverty.
They might tell me I'm not pro-black because of the white people in my circle,
But the preservation of our lives is a top priority.
I'm too introverted to be amongst the people,
Yet I don't want to be alone.
I don't quite fit in with my family members
So I never really feel at home.
I write and I write but words never escape my mouth.
My question is where exactly do I fit into this world?
The answer is I don't.

Frustration.

Sometimes I yell at my children even though they don't deserve it. Thoughts come to mind that I immediately have to push out. I'm okay on the outside. But my mind is unsettled. I constantly overthink on what ifs and should haves. Damn, I wish I could have done or said things differently. But I can't.

I'm frustrated that I've let so many opportunities pass me by. I'm inconsistent. I doubt myself. It's not the right time. Wait until I am more. Wait until. I'm better. I'm frustrated that I'm scared to be in love. Always looking for the one. Never giving him the chance to become.

I push people away. I'm in my own world. I need help but I restrict myself from reaching out. Depend on no one. I love my own company yet I'm frustrated I am alone. No one is to blame. I take full responsibility for the level of my internal and external happiness. I get so frustrated at times.

My mind spins. My head hurts. I lose the ability to focus. My body is on autopilot. It's crazy because I give love, kindness, happiness, encouragement, and understanding freely and openly. My contentment lies in the assuredness that everyone else around me is thriving. My spirit is welcoming and nurturing and yet weary from the limitations I have put on myself.

I know I am exactly where I should be yet where I am is not enough. My purpose won't allow this to be it. My calling. My truth. Won't allow me to be unseen or silent. My spirit...it's shouting. It's frustrating. I'm afraid. That even though I want to be all that I am destined to be I may lose myself in my own mind before I have the chance...

A Caged Bird

Have you ever been asked why a caged bird sings?
It sings because it is trapped.
It sings to be free.
Maybe my silent tears are the songs of a caged bird.
Trapped in her own life.
Imagining the life she can live once her wings are spread wide.
And she can soar.
High...
High above broken promises and shattered dreams.
High above poverty and the shackles of generational patterns.
High above her own limiting beliefs and thoughts asking her how can you fly!?
You've never been free enough to jump and flap your wings!
I sit quietly, peering through the bars of my confined mind.
Waiting patiently for my moment.
Quiet cries.
The melody of my spirit.
One day I WILL be free.
One day I WILL fly!
ONE DAY I WILL SOAR!!

The Fire Within

I want to cry. Not because of some external factor. I'm tired. No, I'm fed up. I am frustrated! I have reached a pivotal moment in my life. Everything in me is telling me this is my moment! This is my calling! This will be the thing to pivot me into my greater life. Everything in me wants this dream...this passion of mine to manifest into reality. I can't eat. I can't sleep. I can't focus on work. This dream consumes me daily. Relentlessly every day at the forefront of my mind.

Have you ever had this feeling in the pit of your stomach? Something deep. Soul deep. Spirit deep. If I don't do this I will die deep! That is exactly how I feel about writing. That is exactly how passionate I am about my craft. About my gift. About my purpose. This dream of mine will change my life. More than that. This dream of mind will save my life! I can't do anything else. I couldn't live with myself.

I need to make this happen more than anything. Now, more than any other time. I don't know what's in store for me. All I know is that I owe myself my best chance. I owe myself the best version of myself. I owe myself this life. I deserve it. I want it. I need it.

It's hard. Mentally and emotionally draining. Knowing very well the potential you have buried just below the person you see every day. It's hard knowing that you are the only one in your family to chase dreams this big. It's hard coming from a family that's afraid to go after dreams. No one can show the way. This is a journey I must begin on my own.

It's like fighting in a ring by yourself. But I'm going to fight nonetheless. Every single day I'm going to fight depression. I'm going to fight poverty. I'm going to fight dependency. I'm going to fight generational toxicity. I'm going to fight mental, emotional, and physical abuse. I'm going to fight addiction. I'm going to fight for my kids. For my nieces and nephews. For my parents. For my siblings. For grandparents. I'm going to keep fighting everything that has held my family back for generations. This isn't about me. This is bigger than me. This is my purpose. Because if not me then who?

Tell Me

Tell me how many times should I dream to make it a reality
Tell me how to turn them into destiny
Tell me the life I live is not all that is destined to be
Tell me my future is close to me
Tell me the pain I've endured will be worthwhile
I feel myself going astray, tell me where to go now
Which steps and how
Which way is up because I've been stuck at down
Tell me to keep pushing, tell me don't stop
Tell me if I keep going I'll make it to the top
Tell me the sun will come as the rain goes
Tell me after this hurricane I'll see a rainbow
Tell me my time is coming, tell me to not give up yet
Tell me this chapter is over and my happiness is next
Tell me to elevate, grow and keep up with my progression
Tell me I'll be proud of myself
Tell me I've learned the lessons
Tell me no more secrets
Tell me no more lies
Tell me I don't have to hide all of me that dwells inside
Tell me I don't have to be afraid and I don't have to cry
Tell me everything is going to be alright
Because I'm telling you the same in the words I write

Growth

"Growth is painful. Change is painful. But, nothing is as painful as staying stuck where you do not belong." — N. R. Narayana Murthy

Self Reflection

I have come to realize there is a blurred line between love and codependency. I have only known codependency, not actual love. I love you because I need you. If I didn't need you I wouldn't love you.

I was used to this form of relationship. I considered myself a healer or helper. Hero complex. Needing to feel needed to stroke my ego. I don't know how to be in a healthy relationship. I've never been in one.

I've sabotaged possibilities to find someone more in need of comfort, guidance, and direction. I thought relationships were about constantly proving my loyalty. How much can I be there without question? I never got the same in return.

In the end, I only received heartache. Disrespect. Entitlement. Failed attempts. Same spirit, different bodies. It's been a while now, and this time I am aware of my preferences and patterns.

I am breaking old cycles that no longer serve me. I no longer choose detriment. I no longer choose codependency. I am not looking for someone who I can "complete" or "heal" or "save" or "change". I am not looking.

I only search for myself. Bits and pieces of me that I've forgotten, I find again. Who or what is in store for me is unknown. I'm okay with that. I may not know what a healthy relationship looks or feels like. But I have learned everything it is not. I am in no rush. Life is a beautiful mysterious journey after all. Until then I love myself enough to never go back to whom I used to be.

I also realize I was selfish. Not monetarily, but selfish with revealing who I really am. My gifts. My purpose. The real me. Before I took this hiatus, I wanted to be a light. In a world so dark. So ready to spread negativity. So ready to tear a person's personality and character and reputation down to nothing over mistakes and decisions we all inevitably make. To be honest, I became that light true enough. I loved to spread love and light. I still do.

But I was afraid I wasn't being real enough. I didn't show people that I hurt, I cry, I struggle. I go through everything everyone else does. A lot of times alone. Because I had gotten so used to showing up with a cape. I didn't know how to fly without it. I didn't show the world that sometimes I needed to be saved too.

So I decided that when I came back I was going to be normal. I was going to fit in. I was going to laugh and joke and curse and post whatever I wanted just like everybody else. This time people would see the real me...but has it been...the real me?

Or have I allowed the world and society to pressure me into the idea that being openly belligerent and thoughtless is okay? I still wasn't okay with who I'd become. The thing is yes I'm human but I'm not normal. I've wandered about this world like a fish out of water most of my life. Not sure where I fit in. Not wanting to.

I carry the weight of the world in my heart. A blessing and a curse. I feel hurt and pain deeply and passionately. I feel wholeheartedly for humanity. The cape fits me. But I know sometimes I have to take it off. I know I can't save everyone. I also know some don't want to be saved. I wish I could save everyone but I can't. And that's okay too. But I can do something.

From here on out. I choose to live as freely and authentically as I can. I choose to be openly expressive in all of my glorious creativeness! God has given me a gift to create and love. Truly love unconditionally. Myself and others. I am simply here to create beautiful art you can hear, see and feel. Nurture. Build. Empower. Enlighten. Understand. I was meant to be a light amid the world's shadows. This is who I am. This is who I want to be. This is who the world needs. No more being selfish. I realize I don't have to become, because I AM.

China Doll

She was beautiful once
A porcelain doll
She was innocent and happy
Delicate
She was meant to be adored
Handle with care
But then placed in careless hands
They never knew her value
Never seen her worth
Life went on
She became tattered and worn
Cracks and scars
Just a shell of what was
Neglect and abuse show clearly now
She is damaged
Fragile
But still imperfectly beautiful
Feel her sacredness and hold her close and tight
But please don't drop her
She will surely shatter and break

Yesterday, Today, Tomorrow

Yesterday didn't exist. It's a memory. A play on consciousness. Teetering on the lines of illusion and imagination. There is nothing you can do to fix or change yesterday. If it is broken it will always be broken. Where there is heartache there will always be heartache. And happiness plays over and over in a time loop. The best you can do with yesterday is keep the lessons and experiences you've gained to better your understanding of today. Honestly, I try to forget most yesterdays...

Tomorrow is my favorite day. I often find myself daydreaming of tomorrow. Wishing, hoping, praying for a better tomorrow. Tomorrow will always be better than yesterday because tomorrow brings hope, faith, chances, and possibilities. Even though it is never guaranteed I love the idea tomorrow brings. I love the mystery. Tomorrow is what keeps a lot of us going, trying, and believing. We believe we will always have one more day to make life worth living. Because if you knew for a fact you didn't have tomorrow would you even try today?

There's a saying that today is only yesterday's tomorrow. Today is the only time that exists. The most important of days is today. It is the only day you can take action. It is the only day you get to decide who you are. It doesn't matter who you were or what you did yesterday. It doesn't matter who you want to be or what you want to become tomorrow. Yesterday is over. And tomorrow is always coming. Today is most special to all humanity. To all things universal. Today is the only day that matters. Today is the only day you can change something. Say something. Start something. End something. DO. SOMETHING. Today is the only day you can BE. What will you do with your today?

Take Me Away

Take me to a place where deep wounds and old scars heal.
To a place where I'm strong enough to coexist with my pain.
A place where I'm not insane and I can begin to feel.
And being in love isn't so surreal.
That's where I want to go from here.
Oh, how I wish there was a place I could go.
I've dreamt about the other side once or twice.
I close my eyes and daydream of a place of true and unconditional happiness.
I hope it's not just wishful thinking.
Take me to a place where I don't have to be strong.
And I can take down the wall I have built for so long.
Take me to a place where my spirit can soar and my wings can spread and my feet can stand firmly on the ground and become one with the roots that nourish me.
Where the sun touches my face and I am completely aligned with all that is.
Take me to a place where emotions run as deep as the oceans and high as mountain ranges.
Someone told me this is where the broken go to unite, heal and grow.
And you have to be taken there, you can't go on your own.
When you're your most brokenness a hand reaches out and chance is given.
And it's scary at first uncomfortable even.
But the hand that reaches out is strong enough to hold you.
Take me to that place.
Take me to the other side of past trauma and repressed memoirs.
Aren't you tired of reading my pain?
I wanna go where a completely different story is written and waiting for me.

Where new chapters and happily ever afters go to play.
Take me away.
I hear it's so worth it to finally reach this special place.
But in the meantime, I'm willing to wait...

A Collage of Butterflies

Blue skies
Beautiful colors
The sunrise
I smile
Happiness is all I feel
Like a collage of butterflies

Like raindrops
Off a rose a pedal
Like ocean waves
Crashing along the shore
My heart now beats
Full of love
Like a collage of butterflies

Dreams of flying
Now realized
I lay amongst the clouds
And land on
A ground of feathers
Like a collage of butterflies

Songs of a robin
Whispers of the trees
It feels like a collage of butterflies
Inside

Who Am I?

She is a goddess.
I am every ancestor that has died before you.
I am the inner voice you have been longing to hear.
I am the whisper of guidance when your sense of direction is lost.

She is energy.
I am everything and yet nothing you can comprehend.
I am everything working together for the greater good.
I am Universal Law.

She is a queen.
I am she who bestowed this crown upon your head.
I am sovereign.
I am the divine purpose of all your thoughts and dreams.

She is elemental.
I am the power of the ocean raging and relentless.
I am the winds and fire of North East South and West.
I am the Mother Earth deeply rooted in all there was, is, and will ever be.

She is life.
I am the giver of all breath that walks this earth.
Through me is the portal of the past, present, and future.
I am her.

Time To Heal

"As my sufferings mounted I soon realized that there were two ways in which I could respond to my situation -- either to react with bitterness or seek to transform the suffering into a creative force. I decided to follow the latter course." — Martin Luther King Jr.

Self Reflection

I began to think I was chasing after and looking for a feeling that doesn't exist. Have I grown accustomed to seeing the "movie love" so much that it is what I anticipate? My whole adult life has been a toxic relationship or no relationship at all. Is it wrong for me to search for something new? Maybe I don't know what true love is. Have I ever felt it? Will I know when I do?

I want to be open to receive love. But isn't it wise, considering my past decisions, for me to be cautious now? Attuned to my intuition. I don't want to keep making the same mistakes. I don't want to give into temptation against my better judgment again.

I would very much like to be in a relationship but I feel I am incompatible. I don't sense connection. I don't feel any relationship is right. I don't sense a life partner. Kisses are meaningless. Conversations feel forced. It's me, not you. I began to push everyone close to me away. I ended friendships, relationships, entanglements and anything my spirit rejected.

I longed for partnership and connection but felt annoyed when my personal space was invaded. Maybe I'm overthinking. It's not you, it's me. I'm difficult, I know. Complex. Layered if you will. I thought there was supposed to be fireworks. A tingling sensation. A gut feeling. SOMETHING to let me know I have found the right one. I still felt nothing. My thoughts overshadowed my emotions. Maybe I remain alone because I am searching for a feeling that doesn't exist. Then again, maybe it is time to love me first before I seek to be loved. And maybe I need to heal before I am able to give myself fully to another person. So I took the much needed time to not only learn the lessons of my past but heal from them too.

Dear Future Husband

Could you wait for me? I don't mean to sound selfish. And I hope you can acknowledge that I'm woman enough to tell you I'm not good enough for you yet. I hope you understand that I have to work on myself internally right now. And understand there are flaws I have that need to be worked out.

There is baggage that I must release. There are mental and emotional burdens that are not yours to carry. And I have to work on it all. Please understand that I can't see you right now. My eyes are searching for completion of myself.

That does not mean I don't yearn for you. It doesn't mean I don't think about our future. I just know I can't love you how I know you need to be loved. I can't commit to you when I haven't mastered keeping commitments to myself. Understand that there are goals I have to reach. There are improvements I have to complete.

I'm not satisfied with myself right now. How can I pour from an empty cup? How can I love you? I don't think that I can. Not right now. I don't want to hurt you. I care too much about you to have you feel unloved, unappreciated, or unimportant. You deserve better than what I have to offer right now.

I'm a woman of my word and I stand here promising you if you would just wait for me a little longer. I'll love you with every fiber and energy of my being. I promise I'll be worth the wait. I'll be the woman you need me to be. I'll be the woman that enhances your already wonderful existence.

We will be a team. We will be one. And we build an empire together. Create a legacy. Our works will speak for themselves. Our children's lives will prosper. In the meantime don't give up. Don't give in. Keeping elevating and vibrating higher so that I can match your vibrations. Don't lose hope and don't give up on love. Don't give up on me. I'm here. I just ask that you wait a little while longer.

Ready, Searching, Waiting

I'm waiting for someone. A special someone. Someone who will push me to new levels. Expand me past my comfort zone. Teach me things I could never learn on my own. Increase my intelligence and intuition. Help balance and align my mental, emotional, physical and spiritual being.

He is strong. Confident. Determined. Intelligent. Powerful. Inspirational. Understanding. And when we talk I want to forget time and space. Someone who knows how to communicate effectively. And listens to understand not to react.

He knows what he wants. And where he wants to be. And is working towards his higher and true self. Respectful. Thought-provoking. Insightful. Works toward learning and improving himself. Spiritually and mentally aligned. He is capable of adding to my greatness. Not diminishing it.

Compassionate. Affectionate. Open-minded. Adventurous. Funny. Someone with dreams just as big as mine if not bigger. And a drive to match it. Someone who takes care of his body, mind, and spirit. And assures his woman does the same. I'm not waiting for a boyfriend or just a husband. I'm looking for a life partner. I'm willing to wait as long it takes to find him. And when you know exactly what you want you don't settle.

The Table

This metaphorical table has brought about many debates. You HAVE to bring something to the table! That is how your value is measured in a relationship right? But what if we instead unpacked ourselves onto this table?

So what do I bring to the table? Or rather what am I willing to lay on it? Here, my love. It's not perfect but it is persistent and unwavering if taken care of. Here, my devotion to you, this home, and our family. Here is my submission and willingness to allow you to lead this family into prosperity, peace, growth, and security.

On this table lies, your escape from the burdens society has placed upon you. Here is your listening ear. Late-night intellectual conversations or simple laughter. Here is your permission to be vulnerable. Here, I also made a place to lay down the mask you wear when you leave home. Here is your safe place.

Here, my experiences, my past, my fears, my pain. My insecurities and self-doubt. My secrets. The ugliness of bad decisions. My humbleness in their wisdom. My hopes, my wishes, my dreams... Sorry, there are no superficial possessions on this table. But there is a lot I chose to lay on it. I'm sure this table is strong enough to hold it all. Now looking at all I have brought to the table. Am I valuable enough for you?

Daydreaming

I want to get lost in your love. I want butterflies in my stomach.
And I want my heart to skip a beat. I want everything that love is supposed to be.
I wish I could wake up to kisses and the embrace of strong warm arms.
I just want to feel your heartbeat.
I want to experience everything that is you and all that it means.
I want the scent of you lingering on my skin and bedsheets.
I want to feel you. To think of you is to feel your energy.
Even when we're apart you're still with me.
I want to admire you. Watch you while you dress.
As the glimmer in my eyes reveals the flutter in my soul and the light within my heart shining for you and only you.
That would be a sight.
I want to hold your hand and know that it's no longer you and me but us. We.
We are a team. Where you fall I will succeed.
And I will be there when you need me,
And you can be there when I'm stressed. We are each other's best.
And yes I want the tests.
I want the trials.
I want the time.
I want the smiles.
I want the cries.
I want the pain.
I want the sun and the rain.
I want to FEEL emotions. I'm just hopeful...
But I want you to know that I'm here. And I'm waiting.
I'm not asking you to rush or run to me just promise you won't give up on me.
Promise you're still going to open your heart for me when I come.

Promise me you aren't done with love.
And I promise I won't give up on us.
I promise I'm becoming the woman of your dreams.
Babe please just wait for me.
No, pray for me as I do for you before I go to sleep.
And just watch all of our prayers and dreams will be our reality.
But until then I'm working on myself.
And I pray to God you're working on you.
We'll be together soon,
With each passing of the moon,
And the passing of the sun.
Until that day comes I'll lie here daydreaming of the day
When you and I become one.

A Good Wife

I can't claim to know how to be a good wife because I've never been married. I don't think I know how to be a good girlfriend because I have never been in a healthy long term relationship. All I know how to be is a genuinely good person. And all I want is to find a genuinely good person to share my life with.

It's okay if you've been broken. So have I. It's okay if you're still trying to find yourself and who you were meant to be or if you are going after your purpose. So am I. It's okay to heal together. Grow together. Love together. And it's okay to take the bricks from the wall we have built around our hearts and build together. I don't want to travel this life's journey alone. And I want you to know you don't have to.

Afraid of Love

I could never tell you how I feel. Not because I don't want you to know. It's hard to orally express my feelings. Yes, I am afraid. I'm so scared, not of you...of feeling. Not you. It's me. You seem ready to jump. I'm so afraid to leap. You see I'm the type to fall so I'm always guarded. I'm just protecting myself. I seem hard. But I'm easily hurt. Emotions are scary. Love can hurt so deep. Don't you agree. Doesn't have to be intentional. You ask me what I feel. It feels like death. When you leave me you take my spirit with you. I'm sad. I don't know why. I feel every emotion. You bring them out. You make me feel every emotion I have been running from.

You speak and I listen. I hear you. I'm speechless. Because you're right. I'm fighting a losing battle. But my mind replays failed attempts and it won't let me forget the risk I'd be taking. There is a wall. A wall that has protected me for years now. I've built it stronger every time I recover from heartache. The same wall that turns to sand with every conversation we have. My defenses are crumbling. I'm still trying to protect myself. And I don't have the energy to fight much longer.

You'll win. You know it. I can't help it. I'm trying to escape the emotions. Life is easier when you don't feel. But I'm thinking maybe it's me that needs to be saved. You're the only one that can save me. But will you? Better yet how can you? Please don't do this to me... don't plant seeds that can't be watered. That can't be nurtured. Don't pull the trigger. Don't break down defenses. Don't make me love you. Only to leave me wallowing in the end. Let me live. Let me survive emotionless just a little while longer.

Love

"True love doesn't happen right away; it's an ever-growing process. It develops after you've gone through many ups and downs, when you've suffered together, cried together, laughed together. — Rico Montalban

Self Reflection

It is one thing to learn the lessons of past experiences. It is a completely other thing to heal from them. Once you heal from the traumas of your transgressions, the possibilities of finding true love increase tremendously. But you must first love yourself.

When you finally choose to release the hurt and forgive, not for the person who hurt you, but for yourself, your world begins to change. There is peace on this side. There is happiness, joy. There is acceptance. And you realize you don't have to carry the weight anymore.

I can't help but to think of all the people I hurt because I was hurting. I can't help but to express my deepest apologies for the mishandle of their feelings. I hope in reading this book, there is understanding and forgiveness.

Loving and accepting myself, accepting the things I have done. Knowing that each of my experiences are a part of me and a part of a beautiful story still being written, has been my salvation.

So often we look for someone or something outside of ourselves to save us. We look for completion, happiness, peace, forgiveness, acceptance, and validation in the eyes of others. Not knowing that all we need, all we ever wanted, is already inside of us.

I'm so happy and so grateful for this process. I couldn't see my journey for what it had the possiblity to be, because I focused, so steadily, on the hurt. The release is so awakening. The feeling is undescribable. I'm so eternally grateful.

I look forward to the giving and receiveing of love and all of its wonderful abundance. I dont close myself from love anymore. I'm no longer afraid to feel. Even more I know that I can feel much more than pain and hurt.

I choose to walk in love, light and gratitude everyday. And because of that, love has come to me. I didn't have to search for it. Beg for it. Alter who I am. I didn't have to change my story or rewrite it to be more appealing. I didnt even have to work hard to receive it. It was ready and willing to be accepted in my life when I was ready.

This love is gentle and warm and assuring. This love is confirmation that I could feel all along. This love is strong during the times I don't want to be. This love is understanding, unwavering, and unconditional. This love accepts all of who I was, who I am, and who I have the potential to be. This love embraces my flaws and imperfections because it understands that because of them I am beautiful. And through this love I see all of my love simply being reciprocated.

A Spark

I could have sworn I heard your heart say I missed you the first time you held me. There is a saying that goes you miss most what you never had. All this time I've yearned for your embrace and never knew it. We fear what we don't know. Our connection scares me. I want my heart, mind, and spirit to yield to you in total surrendering. But I am afraid the walls I've built may be too high.

Patience. Please be patient with me. I know that I can love you the way you deserve to be loved. And I pray now that I can open the doors of my innermost being. And allow you to love me the way I need you to. Because for the first time I can hear my heart saying I've missed you too.

Mind. Heart. Body. Spirit.

The moment I realized I am in love with you. How did you do it? What games did you play? What books did you read? What steps did you take?

I think. You took the time. To dwell. To dive. Inside my mind. Questions and answers. You asked them I answered. You learned me. Understand. First what it means to be my friend. My secrets. The lessons. Memories and moments. You listened. Attentive. We talked and debated. Late night conversations. You paid attention to each of my languages. My words. Their intentions. My facial expressions. My body. The silence. The tears I keep hiding. You find it. And say it's alright. Even though I keep fighting. You took the hits. Took the chance that it would lead to this. Thank you.

My heart. Has been guarded. For so very long. I'm used to the cages. Used to the prison. Used to the aloneness I've grown to live in. I told you I'm okay. What you heard was I need you. I told you I don't need anyone. What you heard was don't leave me. The cries I never weep was your cue to just hold me. With each problem, I told you. You said I can still love you. Let me embrace. No, let me console you. You're hurting and don't even know it. You've learned from the pain but haven't healed from it. The wall is so thick because the scars are still showing. You've been with the wrong ones. Let me love you the right way. Then one day. I can give you what you never had. Not the very best man. But promise to love you the best that I can. I know I'm your friend. That to the end. But if and when you're ready to let me in. Your heart I can mend.

Body to body. Skin to skin. Flesh of my flesh. Your beginning my end. Friends...still? Pleasure or lust? Lust or love? Maybe it's both. Maybe it's none. Maybe you use me, maybe you don't. All I know is it feels good just for this moment. No questions. No thoughts. No more running. I just feel you. I just feel us. My mind escapes me. I am at your will. Make love to me baby. This connection feels good. This connection feels right. I don't want it to stop. I need the escape. Take me away. From the pain and the thoughts. Memories. Moments. Experiences. The loss. I breathe deep. You swallow my moans. And we come. Again. And again. Are we just friends...? Or are we now one?

Day by day. Hour by hour. Minute by minute. The time is ours. Space and reality doesn't exist. We exist together as pure consciousness. My spirit has never known this type of connection. I look to you as my blessing. My manifesting. You are proof that my words have power. And the mind can do wonders. I was speaking to you and over you. I had you in my mind clear as day. I wrote about you long before I knew of your existence. You are truly everything I had hoped to manifest. And now my spirit can begin to rest.

Connection

I hope I'm not being too forward. I want to feel your skin on the edge of my fingertips. So strong. So soft. So delicate. I want to draw you into me. I want to feel energy exchanges and vibrational raises. Each moan you hear is my allegiance to you. I promise I'm not trying to be anything more to you than the peace and escape you need to carry the burdens of your day.

I want to feel our mouths dance in unison. Our bodies in instant connection. This is something deeper than the physical. The vision is near perfection. I'm so ready for you to bless me. Ready to be taken there. How I wish you were here. But I'm willing to wait for what's mine. In due time I suppose.

Your vibe is like red wine and satin sheets. Easy like Sunday morning. I love when you talk to me. Your conversation is ecstasy I levitate on every word. All I can tell you is I feel you. I feel you even though you aren't here. I see you in my mind's eye. I breathe deep. I imagine what you smell like. I close my eyes and imagine you by my side. Is this what it feels like to be treated right. Baby, you are something I am not used to.

You got me feeling like this must be a dream. There's no way you can be this good for me. This must be what it means to manifest dreams. I pray I don't mess this up or scare you away. I hope you want to stay despite knowing my failures. Despite the times, you find all of my flaws and imperfections.

I hope you don't leave. Don't try to wean me away when you know you're becoming my addiction. Not when you've shown me what I didn't know I was missing. Not when my body yearns only for your kisses. And not while I'm feeling these feelings I'm feeling. I'm tripping. I've probably gone too far.

I can't imagine what you must think of me. But I promise baby you are more than I could have ever imagined. Just waiting and planning. Hidden in plain sight. Waiting for me to notice you. Allow me to show you my gratitude.

Thank you for being patient. Thank you for not giving up on me. Thank you for your sincerity. And seeing the Queen in me. Breaking down the wall so you can build with me. And dream with me. And heal with me. Thank you for being the friend I need in this spiritual journey.

You mean more to me than you know. More to me than I can orally express. I hope this written sentiment does its best to portray the thoughts, the feelings, the emotions you bring. Everything that's happening inside is because you came into my life and refused to take no for an answer. Now here we are connecting. Rewriting our pages and chapters...

Signed your Queen
To my Sire

Sire the Sun

I see him when I close my eyes
My baby's a whole vibe
And I'm attracted to his spirit
He hit different
This feeling he got me feeling
Unprecedented
I look up high
And wish upon the sky
That all things align
He continues to be mine
I put intentions in the air
Don't ever question why he's here
To my roots, he's my water
No, he's my sun
No, he's my ruler
He's the one
He's my power
He's my Sire
And nobody compares
Past present or future
I'm praying for him
Manifesting
Forward-thinking
Daydreaming
Whatever you do
Please don't wake me
I'm lost in this dream with him

Mind If I Brag

Let me tell you about this man I know.
Beautiful dark chocolate skin from head to toe.
Arms so strong he amplifies growth.
A beautiful heart and a more precious soul.
I love the way this man makes me feel.
NOT like butterflies and tongue ties and the inability to breathe.
More like soul ties and Sunday mornings and a nice cool breeze.
I'm at peace.
Mind if I brag about this man I know.
See I don't believe in coincidences and chance.
I believe in fate yea it was destined we cross paths.
He's silly, he makes me laugh. But more than that,
He makes me think.
He lifts my crown and raises my head when I want to retreat.
He pays attention to the words I never speak.
He's so attentive in his ways.
So enticing by the night thought-provoking in the day.
This man makes me feel safe.
He makes me feel like even if I am afraid I should always walk by faith.
And leap and take the chance
And push myself. Y'all this man!
I woke up this morning thinking about this man.
I need to hear his voice every chance I get.
I need to feel his skin up against my back
As he wraps his loving arms around my waist and buries his face into my neck.
I close my eyes and feel him inhale me. He embraces who I am.
Boy I tell you this man.
I need him yall.
I need him like the Sun needs the Moon. And the moon needs the

stars.
And the Earth needs us both naturally as we are.
I need him like Mother Earth needs Fire and Water.
We bring balance to each other.
And we could probably coexist but we can't thrive without the other.
Together we live in a world all our own.
Our castle, Our throne.
Our kingdom, Our empire.
His peace, My desire.
His Queen, My Sire.

Trust In Me

Even at your lowest, I will love you.
If you're ever feeling weak let me love you back to strength.
I know you've been hurt, allow my love to mend the broken pieces.
Don't be afraid of me I won't hurt you.
Allow me to take away the stress the world has given you.
You have flaws. Let me see them.
Your imperfections make you perfect for me.
You have weaknesses and fears
Let me balance you and pour into you with courage and power.
You deserve to look into my eyes and find true love, compassion, and understanding.
Take my hand and share with me this happily ever after.
Share with me this life's journey.
Share with me experiences, moments and memories.
Share with me laughter, tears, pain, joy, light and darkness.
You say you have been praying for me.
Well, I have been searching for you.
And if you promise to always stay I promise I won't leave you.

True Love

Only moments in the past
Someone asked
What I thought love meant
What I thought it felt like
The questions stumped me
At that moment I realized
I let time pass by
And I had forgotten
What true love felt like
In the years before you
I had only known
Fake love real lust
Not to be confused
With the matters of the heart
Just the magic of a touch
Because of you
I now know what true love feels like
What it sounds like
Every moment with you
Just feels right
And I know you can feel it too
Because with each word you pour into me
I feel my heart healing through you
So thank you, my love
For showing me what love
Truly is

Spirit

"To me, spirituality means 'no matter what.' One stays on the path, one commits to love, one does one's work; one follows one's dream; one shares, and tries not to judge, no matter what. " — Yehuda Berg

Self Reflection

Last night I fell into an abyss. There was darkness. I wandered around. Listening to the voices. Trying to follow directions to the light. Each voice was a different path back to me. Then there was silence. And the only voice I could hear was my own. And only when I heard my voice for the first time did the light begin to shine.

I followed the guidance of my spirit out of the darkness. Is this what it means to be free? You see I painted a picture of who I wanted the world to see. Or who I thought the world needed me to be. Who I thought I was supposed to be. It's overwhelming trying to fit into this box. It's overwhelming trying to control every aspect of my life. Depriving myself of any real pleasure.

For a long time, I couldn't live with myself. I was sure there were two sides to me. Two different personas. I thought I could separate the traits I didn't want the world to see. I could hide my imperfections and give them a name unrelated to the woman I had shown. How can I not show me and consider myself genuine.

My life was void. Without emotion. Just existing in the present. Maintaining my way of existence and well being. Living and happy in the future. I felt the desire to let go. And be me! I'm not this put together. I'm a mess. A beautiful mess though. I'm not society's replica of what a woman is supposed to be.

In silent retrospection, I have realized this IS me! I'm me! They say life is all about balance and now I know. I'm not here to be less than or part of who I am. I'm here to listen to my own guidance and show the world I can be all of who I am and be happy! I've decided I don't want to listen to the world anymore. I've decided to create my own way.

The Mother

Have you ever seen something so beautiful you wanted to cry? Today I felt it. My spirit was happy. My spirit was home. I felt her speak to me, come deeper. Let me surround you with my loving arms and soft music. The trees swayed. The rain dripped from the leaves of the forest. The birds sang and so did the creek. I closed my eyes. I breathed deep and full. Let nature's energy fill me. I let go.

And there was peace. No thoughts. No emotions. No suffering. There was only me and there was only Earth. And it felt so good. It felt so beautiful to be silent and yet surrounded by the melody of the Mother. I fell in love. I was intrigued and curious. I wanted to explore her depths. But only if she let me. She was inviting and warm.

Everything about her felt like home. And her song was sweet and calm. I could hear her flowing waters as I dwelled further into the unknown. I was consumed by her trees. She caressed me with her branches. And I laid with her. Connected to Mother Earth. I was grounded in her roots. And I could feel the cool breeze of her winds. I listened to the babbling of the creek. And I closed my eyes again.

I was home but I knew I had neared the end of my journey. A deep sadness came over me. I didn't want to leave. I could hear and feel the problems of the world again. I felt tears forming. I wish I could stay forever. The most beautiful place I had ever seen....just a walk away. I'll be back tomorrow. I've found my sacred space in the arms of Mother Earth.

Black Mermaid

I was a mermaid once
A part of a fairy tale
The Ocean
She still calls me
And I can hear the melody
Of her waves
I flow with the tides
I close my eyes
And I'm home
Underwater
I breathe deep
As she caresses my hair
I am her creature
Manatees dolphins and turtles
We are the same
I speak to them
They know my name
I was born in the ocean
Perhaps in another lifetime
Beautiful and serene
Mysterious and mesmerizing
The water gives me life
I submerge my darkness in her depths
And she swallows
I emerge from her healing waters
Whole again

The Air I Breathe

The essence of life would not exist without him
He is the sunrise that opens my eyes
He is everything I need to survive
His eyes are my sky
And his soul is my air

I breathe I breathe I breathe
Until my lungs are filled with his energy
My heart beats his love my spirit knows his trust
I inhale his life. I exhale his despair
His soul is my air

His kiss, I miss
I yearn for his caress
His body is my canvas I paint my love on his chest
Leave me and I will suffocate
As much as he will drown

He is my King
I am his crown
The world is our kingdom
The Universe we share
For my love is his ocean
And his soul is my air

Peace

I close my eyes
There you are
I found you
I can feel your love
Your soul embraces mine
I searched for you in my future
I remember you from a lifetime
I saw you in my spirits memories
You were waiting for me too
And you reached for my hand
You bring me closer
And now there is we
We are one
The sun rises in the distance
I was set free today
My spirit flowed and danced on the shore of the ocean
I am made whole
Nothing else exists
I cry
Finally I am where I am supposed to be

Gone Too Soon

This is simply my cadence to a past dear friend of mine who lost his life by a bullet that was never meant for him.

They say life is short. They say, to cherish every moment. They say you never truly know what you've had until it's gone. They say you can never comprehend the ripple effects your actions, or in this case inactions, can cause. Because you didn't speak up. Because you didn't take action when you were suppose to, a life changes. A life could have been saved. They were right.

And now. A bullet took you away. A mistake. It hurts. My heart. Before I could tell you how I felt you left. I'll never see you again. Never get a chance to speak the unspoken. Never get a chance to think the thoughts I haven't thought of yet. They say you regret most things never done. Nothing can be closer to the truth. I regret everything I never did. I regret everything I never said. I regret the time and moments we didn't share.

Now here I lay in the darkest of dark. In the blackest of night. Your picture lay restfully on my heart. Our too few memories play again and again in my mind. Only pain, misery, and grief accompany me. Voices of the past whisper in my ear. I smile, your voice is familiar and warm. I am now a hollow shell. Possessing no more than what was. Life left me when you took your last breath.

My life is gone because for you I lived. I thrived. And now it's all gone. You left too soon because I waited too long. I didn't take the necessary actions to keep you here with me. Maybe if I had just told you how I felt you would be here. In my arms. Consoling and holding me as I lay on your chest. I can hear you tell me everything is going to be alright.

Instead, now you are only in my heart and mind. And I have to settle, suffice, and remain content with life without you. Who would have known of all the ways you'd leave me like this. So permanent and final. No second chance, Who would have known I'd lose a relationship and friendship so suddenly.

As I lay here in my lonely, miserable darkness, I wonder are you thinking of me? Are memories suppressed once you enter a new realm? Are you cleansed of any thoughts of me once you enter your new world and become a new being? With your new life and new love and new existence. Is it too late to talk to you? Can you even hear me? Can you see me here fighting tears, losing a battle I don't have the strength to fight?

I loved you. I love you. I always have and I will never stop! Not for one second. Not for one second, did I dare dream of not carrying you in my heart. Then again not for one second did I ever think I would be writing this letter to you. Never did I think you wouldn't be a part of my life. But you are. You're gone. Too soon. And I can't help but think it's because I waited too long to tell you how I really felt. I'm so sorry.

Outspoken

"There is no time for despair, no place for self-pity, no need for silence, no room for fear. We speak, we write, we do language. That is how civilizations heal." — Toni Morrison

World Reflection

This chapter is unlike the rest because this is my perspective on the world. The society I live in. This is my voice and where I stand. I am a Black Woman. I am a Black Woman with Black children. And a Black family. I have a Black son.

There are certain aspects and actions of this country that I simply can not and will not turn a blind eye to. This chapter of the book is loud and very intentional. Hear me and hear me good. Know where I stand.

This fight I was born into, I don't try to deny it. I don't try to blend in. I don't try to remain unseen. I was born with a target. I was born to be seen in whatever light you choose to see me.

I am not voiceless. My words are loud, outspoken and victorious. I am the voice to those who can no longer speak because they were killed. They were MURDERED, by the hands of a society who whispers their names in apology.

I am speaking on behalf of those who haven't found their voice yet. Those who are afraid to speak. Those you can't speak. It is our time to be lifted and take back what is inherently ours! Freedom, leadership, dignity, morals, businesses, and generational wealth. What is last will one day be first. And until that day comes, the marathon continues.

I Can't Breathe

LOOK AMERIKKKA

Another notch in America's Bible Belt. The hunger steadily grows. The government is greedy for power, police are greedy for blood. And it shows. It's been showing, we've been watching. They recorded it. 8 minutes 46 seconds.

They smile in our faces. We hope for a conviction. No such thing as redemption. Our blood on their hands. Our freedom is gone in the freest of lands. Won't be long until we're all gasping for breath. I'm just saying where the fuck is OUR help?

Where the fuck is the honor? You must feel invincible don't you in the government's armor, under a white privilege umbrella. In your 'superior circle'. And that uniform that's supposed to say no unjust harm. That's supposed to say innocent until proven guilty and justice for all. That's supposed to say we protect and we serve.

I'm sorry I have no sympathy for y'all. No loyalty for the country whose freedom for us never rings. Not when this country can look me dead in my eyes and say they didn't mean it. You mean to tell me 8 minutes and 46 seconds is an accident? Please.

Where is equality? Damn equality, what about human dignity? The right to not die on camera gasping for breath, begging for help, praying for a savior, saying mama I love you seconds from death! This is outrageous! And you question why we riot in rage? Peaceful protests do nothing. You've proved it again. The same scenario, just a different name trending.

At some point, it WILL come to an end. Now the world has 2020 vision again. The fight for our lives will be an everlasting mission.

But at least this time we have more people standing. And fighting. And speaking. But how long will it be before we're no longer trending?

The truth of the matter is, even though I hope I'm wrong, we will never actually ALL get along. I'm saddened to say equality is a lost cause. We have every right to be passionately vengeful. Until the ones who are responsible are rightfully convicted. And I don't mean a slap on the wrist or paid leave. What about their 'accidental' death for the country to see! Ooo and comment and share! Have them on our newsfeed live for the world to see.

Oh no that's barbaric, isn't it? America couldn't handle a tit for tat situation. Why have I been silent? Believe me, it's not because I want to be. I'm trying my best to promote positivity. Spread peace, love, and light. Protect my children and my sanity. But I'm annoyed at the ignorance some of these people portray. I'm just waiting for real action. There's nothing much left to say.

Change

The word freedom is loosely used. We are confused saying you're stuck but you don't want to move.
And you want an opinion but you don't want to choose. You want the money but don't want to pay dues. And every opportunity gained is lost in excuse.
Today every man's a real nigga. Every woman's a bad bitch.
We think entertainment is the only way to get rich.
Women are stripping and using their bodies for rent.
No common sense. Surviving off a dream and a wish.
It's time for a change. We can't let this epidemic persist.
This is not what our ancestors envisioned! Hangings, beating, marches, and burning crosses for nothing!
You take their sweat blood and tears put on you Jays and then crush them.
But I still see hope in the midst of all this destruction.
Maybe with a little luck…fuck it we need a blessing.
And I know you're probably thinking why the fuck is she stressin'.
Our potential is dying. I hope that I can help save it.
Our priorities are misguided. We've been blinded to the reality of how to survive in the lives we reside in.
I see that car you're driving. The clothes you take pride in.
I see all the girls you get because your wrist is blinding.
But what's all that hiding? Deep-rooted issues dwell inside in.
And where's your mind at? No intelligence.
Buried deep under all your superficial possessions.
Smoke and mirrors taken away and you're not worth the life given.
Believe me I know the struggle is real.
Yet and still, you can grow out of being broke. But being poor is instilled.
So you survive without plans. You're just trying to maintain.

Blaming whoever they are. You're just playing the game.
Now you're tired of the pain. No loss. No gain.
And it could all be avoided if you were willing to change.
Our thought processes have been manipulated.
If you show who you really are you're often humiliated.
Exalted. They don't see you as a loss.
If you don't fit in with normal be ready to pay the cost.
The preacher says in a world full of sin you better kneel at the Cross.
But now the preacher that's supposed to lead us is more than often the wolf. Holier than thou hypocrites ready to play the judge.
Thinking they have the right cuz they sin differently than us.
The God I serve is indiscriminate and their judgments
Are not based on certain preferences from race to different ethnicities, religions, prejudiced marriages.
We are all God's people. We are all the same.
But see your brain has been trained to accept that things shouldn't change.
What you've known your whole life is where closed-mindedness remains.
Look around we are sheep following sheep.
You have the spirit of a leader but your mind is still weak.
I'm tired of all the real niggas. Where are the Kings and Pharaohs and Sires?
Enough bad bitches we need Queens and Goddesses an Empress.
Our children are the future which means they are our leaders.
But how can they learn without the parents to teach them?
These are my eyes this is what I see this is my mind this is what I think.
Our generation is doomed if change doesn't come soon.
And we will have no one to blame because the problem and cure is you.
Instead of complaining be the change that you seek.
In a world full of sheep be shepherd and lead.

Dear Black Man,

I see you. You make think you are invisible to your feminine counterparts. And a target to everyone else. But I'm telling you I see the cards you were dealt. By no means am I implying that I could ever feel your pain. You're just trying to maintain trying to live. Trying not to get shot behind the wheel. Trying not to hear the last word KNEEL. Before being shot because the color of your skin makes you guilty of the crime that is seen in the first degree.

I see you. You may think you are alone. But I am here. Look me in my eyes you see your sorrow and my worry are entwined. Generational memories disguised as pride. I need that strength of your forefathers that remained resilient even when giving up or giving in seemed like the sensible option. That strength, that resilience, that power coursing through your veins. The memories of the pain. I see the scars of the whip lacerations hidden from all others except the eyes who had to endure the visions of watching a husband, a brother, a son or a father punished for being Black. I see you.

You don't have to worry I will never leave you. I couldn't possibly be with the privilege of the people who kept you oppressed. Who laughs at your distress. Or let the world know they care but you only if it doesn't disadvantages them. I want you to know with me you have all the advantages. Don't let the world turn you into savages or thugs or a menace to society or whatever they're calling you because before they took you from the land you were born in and turned you into slaves and put a name on your back you had a crown on your head and you were proud to be Black don't be scared to be Black. Embrace your heritage. Not the culture the media constantly portrays but the grace and prestige and godliness that course through your veins. You have the heart of a lion and the spirit of an eagle. They're just trying to keep you blinded. I'm still hoping you can see it. I told you I see you.

I'm saying all this to say just know we are the same. There is someone who will stand with you, someone to say your name. Oscar Grant. Eric Garner. Tamir Rice. Michael Brown. Alton Sterling. Philando Castile. Kalief Browder. Emmit Till. You all still live. And the rest I'm sorry too many to name. May you rest in heaven knowing someone is saying your name. And to those who are here. Still with the weight of the world stacked against you. Know that I see you. And when it seems as though our society has failed you. Our judicial system wants to hide you. I promise I'm right here with you. My duty to stand by you. I will uplift, protect, and guide you. And know I am always your rider.

To My King.
The Black Man.

Dear Black Woman,

You are my friend. You are my sister. You are not my enemy. I am not your competitor. I'm asking us to stop with the drama. What, when, and who saw him. And all of the gossip. No more fighting and bashing each other. It's time we uplift and help one another. You are a light and a way out of the darkness. From you comes all life so breathe life into chaos.

Black Woman! You are a Queen. You are not defined by the man that you can or can not keep. Your worth is unlimited. So don't play yourself cheap. You are not the smoke and mirrors hidden behind makeup and lace front tutorials. You are not the ignorance and wickedness they continue to portray on us. To make it seem like we don't know we are.

Sis! You are so much more than a wife. A mother. A sister. A daughter. You are the essence of Black Magic. And you aren't your body. But your body is power. Able to endure the birth of all our brothers. There's a reason they say it's nothing like a mother. It's nothing like a black woman. *"Some say the blacker the berry the sweeter the juice. I say the darker the flesh then the deeper the roots."* You deserve respect baby, your Black is beautiful. No matter what shade what shape. Your hair. Your curves. Love who you are, girl you got the juice!

Queen! You are not voiceless. And what you say matters! Don't be afraid to say Me Too! Our Lives Do Matter. We have the voice of a lioness. So let your roar be heard! No longer will we remain silent and hidden in the shadows of what society deems unacceptable! Let our voices be heard all over the world. Every grown woman. Every teen. Every girl! We are here, right here in the face of prejudice, sexism, and discrimination. Still strong. Still standing. Still refusing to let life betray us. And for the ones who have fallen may they not be forgotten. This mistreatment and abuse that Black women have to endure must come to end. Where are our girls? Where are our women?

Black Women! We are a community. This is more than a hashtag, this is a movement. Keep stepping, keep moving. And breaking barriers. Climbing social ladders! This is a man's world but nothing would be if we weren't behind it. And for every great man. Know there's a woman behind him. In competition we fall so let's stand undivided. United! Realize how great we all are when we come together. The power we have is indescribable and anything can prosper if we stand as a collective. So wear that crown baby girl don't you dare drop it! This is Black girl magic. The Original Queens! And yaaassss Black girls rock! No matter what you believe. You better know we don't quit and hell no we ain't leavin!!!

To My Queen.
The Black Woman.

Liberation

Red, my ancestors blood.
White, is the skin that beat and killed them.
Blue, is the uniform attached to not one conviction.
Green, the pastures I walk.
Black love is all that rock.
Gold is what we were dripped in before we were trapped and bought.
I'm tired of all the losses,
But giving up is not an option
This marathon continues,
As long as there's still affliction
Take the stick get ready to run,
This race we're in isn't done.
As long as we continue to die,
The torch will be passed on.
It's a revolution! Nah this ain't that kind of poem.
Let me break it down for you to see where I'm coming from.
Now trust me I remember,
It's been fucked up how they did us
Hanging us with wires and nooses,
The burnings of churches and crosses,
Black men incarcerated,
Women used for their body.
With every problem we have,
We're bound to protest behind it.
But hold up for just a second,
Consider a new perspective.
Instead of just looking outward,
It's time for inner reflection.
Quiet the chaos around you,
It's time to think for yourself.

You're looking for a savior,
But we can't pray to the same help.
Their God is not Our God.
It's time that we save ourselves.
It's time we look toward our own instead of to someone else.
I'm talking about liberation.
I'm talking about meditation.
I'm talking about manifesting.
I'm talking about salvation.
Basically, I'm talking about talking to the God in me.
The act of setting me free.
You could be free too,
But your mind is still weak.
We have to raise consciousness,
In order to be released,
From the illusions of the oppressor,
You've known this matrix to be.
We aren't physically slaves,
But there's still shackles on our souls.
Maybe with a little hope, nah this how the story will go.
We will vibrate higher.
We will pick up our crowns.
We will stop all this foolishness and putting each other down.
We will protect our children.
The king's will protect the queens.
We will keep the money flowing,
In our own communities.
We will mind our business.
We will stay in our lane.
We will stop the inner crimes,
And driving each other insane.
We will protect our legacy.
We will prioritize health.
We will stop repeated cycles.
We will preserve our wealth
This is the unchaining of our minds.

Unloosening of our spirits,
Unshackling of emotions,
Untying of our businesses,
Unbinding of all that was.
We will be lifted up.
You want to be liberated?
Well it starts in the mind of us.
You really want to be set free?
That's what's up so do I,
But in order to be set free,
You have to realize freedom is in the mind.

Where Can I Go

I wish there was a place where all people were in unison.
I wish we did not see color.
Or gender, sexuality or religion.
I wish there was a place where people could only see spirit.
I wish we could only see the heart.
I wish I didn't have to fear for my daughter or my son.
I wish my son didn't gain a target for being born.
I wish we did not judge people based on our possessions.
I wish we didn't see material possessions as blessings.
I wish for a place that is not governed by greed and power.
I wish liberty was truly ours.
I wish we did not kill and hunt. Fight and hurt.
Just for entertainment and fun.
And the use of spoken words are like bullets in a gun.
I wish we didn't fear the unknown.
I wish we could collectively rise and grow.
I wish people did not divide themselves based on old books and pictures.
I wish we knew better.
I wish this world was not headed for destruction.
And I wish humans weren't the cause.
I wish I didn't have to cry for this world.
Cry for my people. Cry for my son.
Wishful thinking, thinking there could be a chance.
For all my wishes to come true.
I wish I had the answers.
I wish so much more.
But most of all I wish there was a place I could go...

Afterword

What a journey so far and still a journey to go. Thank you for taking the time to get to know me. Thank you for your support. Thank you for allowing me to express myself in the best way I can, through my writing. Thank you for experiencing this part of my story. Hopefully you would have resonated with some part of this book.

If you've gotten to the end, it let's me know one thing for sure. You ARE consistent. And you CAN persevere. You had to, to reach the end of this book. Growth is inevitable. Change is inevitable. How you change and how long it takes to grow, THAT is up to you. So if anything, I hope after reading this book you realize it's not about where you've been. Where you've gone. Who your family is. What you were born into. It doesn't even matter if you have flaws or feel you're imperfect. We all have a story to tell and through it all you are still worthy to tell yours.

I hope you were able to learn and grow through me. And I hope you understood the messages I attempted to convey in each chapter. As I stated earlier, this journey isn't over for me. In fact this is only the beginning. And as such, I look forward to writing and releasing so much more. It's been a pleasure and a privilege to see this book to fruition. I hope you enjoyed reading it as much as I enjoyed writing and cumulating the story and pieces of my life. May you carry any pieces of this book with you that allows you to vibrate higher, love yourself, find your own voice, and write YOUR happily ever after.

Until the next book family...

About The Author

Trice Lashay

Trice was born on July 10, 1991, in Atlanta, Ga. She has 8 siblings combined. She is the mother of two wonderful children. She is a full-time writer and currently resides in Stone Mountain. She is an avid follower of self-development, spirituality, health, and the elevation of African Americans.

Trice Lashay is also known for her songwriting skills and loves music, she sings as well. She is looking forward to the production of her first single in the near future.

To gain a more personal insight into her life, follow her on:
Facebook - Trice Lashay - Enigma
Instagram - @tricelashay_thewriter

She can also be reached via her website or email:
www.iamroyaltyet.com
tricefoster@iamroyaltyet.com

Made in the USA
Middletown, DE
16 February 2023

25015116R00071